Joy Comes in the Morning

21 Days of Healing Devotions

by

Rev. Alvin G. Blackard, Jr.

Pastor, Northside Assembly of God

PEACE PRESS OF SPRINGFIELD

Peace Press of

Springfield, Missouri

©2015 by Rev. Alvin G. Blackard, Jr.

For queries, contact:

peacepressofspringfield@gmail.com

Text editing by Hestia and Julius

Cover art by Jacek Fraczak

Interior design and layout by Jesse Nickles
jessenicklesdesign@gmail.com
jessenickles.net

Contents

Introduction and Acknowledgments

While walking this earth our Lord and Savior, Jesus Christ, healed the sick in mind, body, and spirit. In the Assemblies of God—the church that I am honored, and humbled, to serve as pastor—we believe that the Holy Spirit remains active in healing those whose faith is nourished and sustained by grace. Beyond His precious gift of the Spirit, God has given His children many arts of healing, not the least of which is modern medicine and its technologies. But, just as we do not live by bread alone, neither can we live—that is, *be fully healed in mind, body, and spirit*—by mere machinery and pharmaceuticals. I don't deny the utility of modern medicine, but I take my stand as a pastor and declare that health cannot be compartmentalized in ways that separate the physical from the emotional and the spiritual.

Holistic practitioners have long assumed a mind-body unity, such that "the mind leads the body" in healing. For those who believe they can't be healed, their belief becomes a self-fulfilling prophecy; but those who stand firm in the belief that they *will* be healed bring God-given powers of intention to bear on their bodily health. From a pastoral perspective, it's a small but crucial next step to declare the triple unity of body, mind, and spirit. The body cannot heal fully without intercession of the spirit; and even the spirit, at times, is in need of healing.

Often, a physical illness has its origins in emotional and spiritual distress or "dis-ease." When this is the case—and it happens far more often than people assume—then prayerful devotion is the most potent medicine any healer can prescribe.

Most people who know me personally also know my wife, Susan Blackard. Among her numerous medical accomplishments, she is an RN who practices holistic healthcare in a local private clinic. We are both healers in our own way; and we share not only the same Christian faith but also the same convictions regarding the body-mind-spirit unity. It has been a blessing to be able to combine our healing faith, as empowered by His Spirit. Of course, *all* the praise goes to God, from Whom all blessings—and healings—flow.

This book of devotions has a double audience. For members of my congregation (and their families and friends) at Northside Assembly, I offer it as a three-week journey in spiritual healing. For clients of Susan's Rejuvenation Wellness Center, I offer it as a spiritual supplement to their physical healing. Originally, Susan's private clinic was named Rejuvenation 21: A Journey to a New You. The name may have changed, but the philosophy remains. Healing *is* a journey that is completed only when the body-mind-spirit are in accord. "An apple a day" is good advice; a devotion a day even better. So, take the following as a 21-day journey toward wholeness, confident in hope and sure of God's guidance. On this journey, you are not alone!

Now, here's a paradox: though this little book offers a 21-day journey, its destination is ultimately a *return*—that is, a return to the health and wholeness God intended for us to begin with. Our lives are a series of cyclical returns. With each midnight, a new day comes. Resting in the Sabbath, each week affords both progress and retrospect: *How have I grown?*—That's one of many questions that I'm challenged to ask weekly … *What have I done for the Lord? What have I done for my congregation, for those whom God has placed in my care? (Oh, and have I finished writing Sunday's sermon?)* In the procession of seasons, Christmas comes, and comes again … and so does Easter …

Like the seasons, our bodies, too, have their cycles. Nightly sleep leads to daily wakefulness. That's our Circadian rhythm at work: we get out of bed in the morning and begin our daily routine, then we return to bed and turn out the light and—hopefully!—awake refreshed to begin a new day. And we do so again, and again. I make this point, because *healing involves cycles, too.* I've written three weeks' worth of devotions for much the same reason that Susan once called her clinic Rejuvenation 21. Conventional wisdom holds that it takes 21 days to break a habit and restore the mind-body-spirit to its prior state. While it can certainly take longer for some people to break some habits, I'm going to assume that 21 days' worth of devotions will get us back to where we need to be—or, at the least, get us "back on track" and pointed in the right direction. (Besides: you can always go back to Day 1 and do the devotions again, and again!)

With each day's devotion, I'll tell a story—sometimes humorous, sometimes serious, often taken from personal experience—and make an application to Scripture. And then, it's the reader's turn to take over. *Use the blank page following each devotion.* Keep pen and pencil close at hand and get in the habit of writing, drawing, doodling … In some manner, try to record your impressions as they arise. Who knows? If you get used to writing in troubled times, you may find yourself writing in ordinary and even joyful times. Creative expression, of the sort that these devotions foster, can become a lifelong habit. (Needless to say, some habits are *good* habits.) As part of your healing, unleash your creativity: it will help free-up trapped emotions. It will also help express the inexpressible—that is, your joyous relationship with the Lord.

Wherever you are on your path to healing, *write about it.* And, in time, you'll find yourself writing about love, and joy, and gratitude, and happiness, and simple peace.

I dedicate this book to the loves of my life:

To my late Mother, Anna Marie, who was there at the beginning of this journey, giving life to me.

To my love and best friend Susan, my wife who brings such stability and reason for being to the depths of my soul. No one could ask for a better helpmate, a woman who approaches life as more than worth living but as giving worth to living. Susan has given of herself to so many in so many ways. She is God's gift.

To my children Nathanael, Anna LaDawn, and Christopher. Never could I have dreamed there was enough love in my heart for all three. But there is far more than enough to include their wonderful families, who gave us beautiful grandchildren. You each are unique, gifted, and special beyond words to me.

And to my Lord and Savior who completes me body, mind, and spirit, a friend who stays by my side, closer than a brother. I desire to live my life in a manner well-pleasing unto Him to hear Him say, in the end, "Well done, thou good and faithful servant."

If I can help somebody along this journey of life, then my living will not have been in vain. To one and all, I thank you for just being you and for enriching my life. We are all on this journey together.

To all readers of this book, their loved ones and friends: I wish you God's love, joy, peace, health, and prosperity.

Rev. Alvin G. Blackard, Jr., Pastor
Northside Assembly of God
Springfield, Missouri
July 4th, 2015

Joy Comes in the Morning: 21 Days of Healing Devotions

"Do not fear, Daniel, for from the first day that you set your heart to understand,… your words were heard; and I have come because of your words. But the prince of the kingdom of Persia withstood me twenty-one days; and behold, Michael, one of the chief princes, came to help me…"

—Daniel 10.12-13 (NKJV)

Weeping may endure through the night, but joy comes in the morning.

—Psalm 30.5

Day 1.
Daniel's 21 Days of Fasting

Congratulations on beginning your journey to a new you, restored in body, mind, and spirit!

I take the title of this chapter from a passage in Daniel 10.10-13 (NKJV):

> Suddenly, a hand touched me.... And [the angel] said to me, "O Daniel, man greatly beloved, understand the words that I speak to you, and stand upright, for I have now been sent to you."...

> Then he said to me, "Do not fear, Daniel, for from the first day that you set your heart to understand, and to humble yourself before your God, your words were heard; and I have come because of your words. But the prince of the kingdom of Persia withstood me twenty-one days; and behold, Michael, one of the chief princes, came to help me, for I had been left alone there with the kings of Persia."

Here, an angel visits Daniel to give him the vision he had prayed and fasted for. For 21 days, Daniel prayed and fasted, fasted and prayed. And, while he prayed and fasted in his flesh, a spiritual battle—waged across those same 21 days—was being fought by God's angel against the "prince of the kingdom of Persia." Let's apply this scene to our own lives. God may not call you to battle against the kings of Persia, but you do have your own internal battles. Our foes come in many forms: in habits of lifestyle, in toxic thought patterns, in spiritual malaise. But the angel—God's messenger—came to tell Daniel "his words were heard."

Daniel's words were prayerful. In pastoral care, we teach the power of earnest, persistent *prayer*, in healthcare, which is my wife's vocation, they teach the power of *intention*. What we've learned as a team over the years is that these words may differ but their desired effects are the same.

Prayer is a form of intention that directs our passionate attention toward God. Until we tell God—and those to whom He has entrusted our care—what we wish and intend for ourselves, our will power remains unstrengthened, unsupported, and disengaged. In other words, prayer is our best means to make our intentions "real."

The angel was sent to Daniel, but the "prince of the kingdom of Persia" (call him Satan, if you will) tried his hardest to delay the messenger and his message. And, for many of those days of spiritual warfare, the victory seemed in doubt. In your healing journey, that will be true for you, too: there will be days when the foe seems to get the upper hand. But, as the angel tells Daniel, *"from the first day that you set your heart to understand,* your words were heard." Think about it: Daniel's victory was assured from the moment that he expressed his prayerful intention.

In my own life, I take Daniel's experience to heart. The victory and the vision was already his, but he had to fast and pray for it—for 21 days, in fact. For many readers, 21 days might seem merciful, given the difficulty and duration of some illness. But consider that the spiritual battle being waged on Daniel's behalf was all-out, life or death, light vs. darkness. I cannot help but think that Daniel's 21 days of praying and fasting in the flesh were somehow tied to that cosmic struggle between the forces of light and darkness. One thing I'm certain of is that we are never alone in our mourning, our fasting, and our praying: our own physical struggles have cosmic implications, so God sends His angels and even His Son, Christ Jesus, to fight on our behalf. It's not the number of days that count, it's the promise of a victorious end.

Think about your own foe now, whether it be physical or emotional or spiritual (or, more likely, a mixture): say to yourself, "The victory is mine, though I remain in the field of battle."

And the angel tells Daniel that it was another greater champion, the archangel Michael, who won the victory against the forces of darkness. The point is that victorious healing is never entirely our own—*though it begins* with our prayerful intention. Had Daniel not asked, he would not have received. And, having asked in the right spirit, his victory was assured. But that victory was neither easy nor immediate. While the spiritual battle raged above, Daniel did his own part below, fasting and praying, praying and fasting.

Can you see how Daniel provides a model for understanding our own battles with dis-ease of any sort? Express your intention—affirm that you *will* be healed—and embrace the fact that victory comes … *in time*, and with the help of angels.

Let's shift metaphors now, from warfare to journeying. Our desire for health of any sort—physical, emotional, or spiritual—places us on a path that can be difficult at times to walk. Side roads tempt us; it's too easy to slack off our pace and to pause, even leave the path temporarily—maybe even leave it altogether.

Many people think of healing as a passive affair, as something that *happens to* them, not as something they have to pursue consciously, strenuously, confidently. These people look for their ship to come in—but they never sent one out! You, in contrast, are sending your ship out by means of your conscious, prayerful intention *to become the person you want to be*—a person of health in body, mind, and spirt—just the way that God intended you to be. Stay the course, and your ship will come in.

So, I'm writing this first of 21 daily devotions to encourage you to fight the fight—and to stay the course. As you set out on your path, learn to fight the temptations to stray. When you come across roadblocks, sidetracks, and setbacks, just remember: by prayerfully concentrating your intention on the task at hand, you *will* reach your journey's end.

Take each step one at a time, one day at a time, for however long it takes.

And remember: to heal, you must make healing a *conscious* intention. Many people are unaware of this fact: they say they *want* to heal, though their faith is weak. But, if you draw on the loving support of the angels that surround you—both human and divine—and resolve that *healing is your birthright, destiny, and destination,* then nothing can stop you!

Be like Daniel!

And remember how he prayed for a vision from heaven and, after 21 days, the angel came: "*from the first day that you set your heart to understand,...* your words were heard."

Wow! What a Triumphant end for Daniel, who never gave in or gave up. Triumphant: that's "TRY with UMPH." Practice this throughout the day: put some *umph* in your trying.

1. It's Your Turn to Reflect and Write. "As a man thinks in his heart, so is he" (Proverbs 23.7). Actually, Proverbs 23 warns against bad habits of eating as well as of thinking. You've heard the phrase, "you are what you eat." Proverbs reminds us that "you are what you think," too. So, let's take Solomon's admonition as the first step on this first day of our devotional journey together. Don't let old or bad habits of thinking define you! Instead, *learn to think differently*, particularly about your physical-spiritual health. Repeat to yourself, "I *will* be healed. God wills me to be healed. My healing has begun. And I thank God for putting me on this path."

Also, as you begin this journey, take time to reflect on your goals. Write down each of the battles that you're currently waging within: and after each, write, "the victory is mine through God." It's just a matter of time.

18

For your writing:

Day 2.
"And the Sun's Coming Up in the Morning"

In this second day of devotion, your task is to be mindful of the blessings of each new day. "Weeping may endure through the night, but joy comes in the morning" (Psalm 30.5). Let every day be a new beginning.

I remember when my wife Susan and I had finished a weeklong mission outreach to the Apache Indians in Arizona. We had taken a team to put a new roof on the missions church and do some interior remodeling. That was all for the health of the body; for the spirit, we conducted daytime Bible studies and led evening community outreaches of music. We shared much from our hearts during that week.

My wife and I had prepared a course (with teaching guides) titled "The Power of Love." And yet, it wasn't so obvious at times just who were the teachers and who the students. I remember being humbled by one of our new friends, who said, "In the Apache language, there is no word that renders love, as love is only a word. True love must be expressed and shown, not merely spoken." It took a moment or two for his words to sink in. Properly so-called, love *can't* be a word merely—a sound from one's lips rather than actions from one's heart. Lacking heart and action, the word "love" is meaningless.

So we took that insight to heart through the rest of our week's mission: we aimed to *do* love, not merely speak it.

When the week came to an end, our mission team piled into the church bus for the ride back to Springfield. It's not much of a vehicle, being an old converted school bus; but it wasn't "built for show." After all, it's Godly love and actions that define a church, not the expense of its vans and buses. We were all ready to return to our normal lives, so we planned to drive non-stop through the first night. The bus had no air conditioning, but we didn't need it. With windows open, we drove through the desert, uplifted by a week's worth of love-in-action. We felt the dry Arizona winds intermingling with the winds of the Holy Spirit, and our exhilaration lingered well into the night as we journeyed back home.

By the early morning hours, the passengers had managed to find comfortable enough positions for sleep. I was driving and all was silent about me, except for the rushing air and the steady hum of the engine. As I drove, I reflected on the people whom we had come to serve and come to love, and I counted the many gifts that we had received and some that we had given.

And with the approaching dawn, day 1 of our journey back home was making its turn into day 2.

Sunrise in the desert: what can be more beautiful? For company, I turned on the radio. And, just as the first rays of dawn broke forth, a song came on. It was "And The Sun's Coming Up In The Morning," written by Ila Gaskin and recorded by the Rex Nelson Singers:

> Once again, I face Satan this morning,
> And I battle him all the day long,
> But in my weakness, God sent reinforcements.
> And at sundown, I'll sing victory's song.

> And the sun's comin' up, in the morning
> Every tear will be gone from my eye,
> This old place is gonna give way to glory,
> And like an eagle, I'll take to the sky …

As I drove, the music reintroduced me to the breath-taking visionary scenes of an open desert stretching out to the horizon, where the sun rose in all its magnificence.

Thrilled by immense beauty of God's creation, I thought back to the community we had just left—a community that lived in poverty, yet lived proudly and appreciatively. The people there had opened their homes, their house of worship, and their customs to us. And, in God's presence, we met on common ground: made in the image of our Creator, we were all one in the Lord. Their lives, their world, were as rich and valuable as any king's.

And so, on this second day of meditation, I remind you what my Apache fellows in Christ taught me: that *love* is more than a word. And though churches need roofs and mission teams need buses, it's the people that we minister to that count: people are the main thing in life.

And remember that after the night, "joy comes in the morning."

On this second day of your healing journey, why not "roll down your windows" and "feel the breeze"? Nature is restorative, so look for ways to feel God's creation—and remember that *you are part* of His glorious creation, made in His image. And remember that *your* journey intersects with others' journeys in joyous ways. Above all, remember to *turn love into action*: make it more than a word.

When you look for the dawn and look for God in nature and look for God's image in others, the love that will be unleashed will have its own healing effects. *You cannot heal yourself until you help in the healing of others.* Let this second day be the dawning of your rededicated life in love.

2. It's Your Turn to Reflect and Write. Through-out this second day of devotion, take solace in the beauty of God's creation—remembering that *you* are a blessed part of that creation. Make a list of people and places that you love. If you have the time, go somewhere "off the beaten path."

And commit to *do* something beautiful and loving: for yourself, for your neighbors, for God. Preach God's Word—and *sometimes use words!*

For your writing:

Day 3.
Let Go and Let God

Whoever calls on the name of the Lord shall be saved. (Romans 10.13)

Jim loved to spend time in nature, surveying God's creation, and hilltops were his favorite vistas. Needless to say, Jim was an experienced hiker. So one fine summer's day Jim got in his truck and headed out to a mountain that had long beckoned him. Hills he could conquer with ease; but the mountain trail was steep and he found himself in unfamiliar territory. Still, it was a pleasant hike up and the view from the mountaintop was spectacular—well worth the trip. And so, after a full day's hiking, he headed back down the trail to his truck. But as he hiked down the steep and narrow trail, the sun set behind the mountain and he found himself trying to negotiate in the dark.

Not knowing the trail, Jim felt his foot slip out from under him. He fell on his backside and started sliding down the slippery rock surface, which took him to the edge of a cliff—and over he went. Flailing about with his arms, he felt a sapling near the cliff top and managed to grab hold of it. It bent under his weight but its roots held firm. And he held on for dear life, yelling for help though no one was there. The thought came to him that no one could hear his cries for help.

Hours passed and still he hung on in the darkness. You might say that Jim was a stubborn young man who was going to put his stubbornness to use. He would hang on, he decided, until he was completely without strength in the hope that, just maybe, someone would hear him and help.

As the hours went by, he thought of his family, his friends, his dreams. But he knew he couldn't hold on much longer, so he made his peace with the Creator. And as he prayed, he heard a voice say, to his surprise, "*Let go, Jim.*"

It wasn't the voice that surprised him so much as what it said. "Let go?!" he yelled out loud. "Are you kidding me? And fall to my death?" But again the still, small voice said, "*Jim, let go.*"

Jim refused, but as the strength ebbed from his body he could no longer hang on, and so he did let go. Not in obedience to the voice, but out of sheer exhaustion.

To Jim's surprise—and inexpressible relief—he fell a distance of twelve feet. It wasn't that much of a cliff after all, and he found himself lying in a bed of moss covering a wide, safe, and easily walkable ledge. For hours he had been clinging to that sapling and, all the while, safety lay a dozen feet below him.

And for a third time he heard that still, small voice: "Jim, I had you covered. All you had to do was *trust.*"

Jim went for a hike and took a lesson in faith. He prayed and his prayer was answered, but he didn't trust the voice and its advice. He was so used to doing things his way that he couldn't "let go" and give himself over fully to God's care. But when he did let go, God's open hand was waiting underneath, ready to catch him.

On this third day of your journey, it's time for you to let go. If you want to know what impedes your progress, ask yourself, "What am I holding on to?" The fact is, we hold on to our worries and fears and old habits and prejudices, just like Jim clung to that sapling: we're a pretty stubborn species, after all. But when we let go, God will keep us and provide.

There's another lesson that Jim's story teaches us, and it's the single most important lesson of this book. In times of trouble, call on the name of the one who can help you. He is faithful and is there before you get there, and He will be there after you are gone. Call on the name of Jesus. If you call on His name, He will save you and guide you. But, until you call on His name, you'll be hanging from a limb off a cliff, having lost your footing and fallen off of the path.

3. It's Your Turn to Reflect and Write. Throughout this third day of devotion, reflect on what's been holding you back. Much of what's holding you back is what you're clinging to, refusing to let go. Our healing path is often mountainously steep and narrow, and the sun sometimes sets on us, leaving us in darkness. But if we let go and call on the name of the Lord, we'll be placed back on the path, safely.

So spend the day calling on Jesus. And make an inventory of all the worldly things you're holding on to.

When you've compiled your list, turn it into a series of affirmations:

Today, I let go of …

Today, I let go of …

Today, I let go of …

And then really and truly *let go*.

For your writing:

Day 4.
Just Show Up

The Upton Volunteer Fire Department was made up of retired men and women from all walks of life. Their small town needed a fire company, so these folks stepped up and took the challenge.

They enjoyed their times together at the fire station and at picnics and community functions. They were pretty good at fighting fires, as well, considering their fire truck was an old La France Engine, built in the early 1900s. But it was theirs and they took pride in cleaning and polishing it, making her look her best.

One day an emergency call came into the Upton Volunteer Fire Department. There was a large fire in a town nearby that needed all the help it could get. A manufacturing plant that had done business in the community for years was burning, and many families depended on it. So the alarm was sounded and calls were made, and soon Upton and her volunteers were on their way.

Meanwhile, at the scene of the blaze, two other local volunteer fire departments had arrived. But the fire was so intense that the firefighters stood helplessly outside the front gates. "It's already an inferno," they said, "and we're only volunteers! Do you expect us to risk our lives?"

Soon, the plant's owner arrived. Seeing the out-of-control blaze and realizing that the machinery inside his plant—the biggest employer in town—was on the verge of destruction, he shouted out a desperate offer: the fire department that entered the gates and put out the fire would receive a $100,000 donation from him personally.

Still, no one moved. No fire engine advanced. The danger was too great.

And then, in the distance, the plant owner heard a windy, whistling sort of siren that could mean only one thing: the Old La France was coming and, with it, the Upton Volunteer Fire Department. Presently, the single light above the Old La France windshield was coming into view and—oh! what a sight!—the old retirees were barely hanging on, some of them still buckling on their helmets (with fringes of silver hair rustling in the wind) while others clung to an inner railing and wrenched on their boots. The firefighters at the scene chuckled at the sight; some laughed out loud as the old engine roared by.

But, as the Old La France approached the plant's front gate, no one could have guessed what happened next. The old engine didn't slow down a single mile-per-hour—if anything, it was gaining speed—and, with the old folks hanging on for dear life, the Old La France made a mighty crash right through the gate, strewing debris into the air that fell behind them like chunks of wooden rain, scattering the local firefighters into the bushes.

And the Old La France kept rolling. Making its way right up to the front door, it jumped the curb and screeched to a halt right in front of a fire hydrant. The locals, who had rallied and ran behind the Old La France, were ready with a hose. In the meantime, the old-timers eased themselves off the old engine, grabbed their gear, and disappeared into the billowing smoke.

It was a two-hour all-out war, fighting this fire, but the Upton Volunteer Fire Department kept moving doggedly, as if "stop" was not in their vocabulary. *No doubt many of these good men and women are veterans*, thought the plant owner, marveling at their effort. Gradually, the fire was subdued and at last vanquished, to the supreme relief of the owner.

A rousing applause rose from the crowd and continued to grow in volume as the dirty, exhausted, bent-over Upton volunteers emerged from the smoking building. One by one, they dragged their aching bodies over to the Old La France and, laughing quietly and smiling among themselves, they collapsed into its capable arms.

When the crowd had quieted, the plant owner came forward and spoke in a loud voice, so everyone could hear: "Thank you—thank you members of the Upton Volunteer Fire Department, for your bravery today, for your loyalty and your great valor in throwing caution to the wind and, contrary to logic and all common sense, hurling yourselves at the fire, risking death to save a sizeable and very valuable portion of my company's building. I cannot thank you enough. But to try, I'm going to honor my word and, tomorrow, the Upton Volunteer Fire Department will receive a check from me in the amount of $100,000. Thanks again, and congratulations."

There was a second round of applause, at which the Upton Fire Chief struggled to his feet and went up to the plant owner to shake his hand.

"So, Chief," said the manufacturing man after the crowd had settled. "$100,000 is a lot of money!

What do you think you'll use it for?"

Without much thought the Fire Chief replied, "Well, I guess, first we better fix the brakes."

Though a light-hearted story, the Upton Volunteer Fire Department teaches us two lessons. The first lesson is obvious: there are times when you need to go "all out," like the Upton volunteers. "Putting on the brakes" can slow your healing, and fear can bring progress to a halt. Don't let anything slow you down on your path to healing. Just trust in God, rev up the engine, buckle yourself in, and head down the road!

The second lesson is a little less obvious, perhaps. Sometimes the key to success is simply *showing up*.

Challenges arise and, even when circumstances lie beyond your control, you may find opportunities to serve in ways you could never have dreamed possible. What the world calls chance is in fact God's handiwork, so you'd best be ready to roll up your sleeves and dig in when opportunities arise.

For a Scriptural example, consider Joseph son of Jacob. Talk about being buffeted by fortune! His jealous brothers sold him into slavery; but, once in Egypt, his industry led to his promotion as overseer of his master's properties. And when he ran from his master's wife's advances, he was falsely accused and thrown in prison. But, even in prison, his industry led to his promotion. Despite continuous betrayals, Joseph "showed up" and rolled up his sleeves. And, as it turns out, Joseph was being used by God. For it was in Egypt, and under Joseph's conscientious care, that the tribes of Israel were founded.

In fact, Joseph's life-journey was *always* in God's hands, even when it didn't look like it, "because the LORD was with him, and that which he did, the LORD made it to prosper" (Genesis 39.23).

So, on this fourth day of your journey, be like Joseph!

4. It's Your Turn to Reflect and Write. Throughout this fourth day of devotion, reflect on the ways that God's handiwork has appeared in seeming "accidents" and chance events in your life.

Then write of a time when you "showed up," rolled up your sleeves, and made a difference in people's lives. Consider how helping others, even in unexpected circumstances, can contribute to your own healing.

For your writing:

Day 5.

Casting a Net in Florida

Then Jesus said to them, "Children, have you any food?"

They answered Him, "No."

And He said to them, "Cast the net on the right side of the boat, and you will find some."

(John 21. 5-6)

I have often remarked to friends that I could sure "Surf the Lord,... I mean *Serve* the Lord" in Florida.

My wife's relatives live in Florida and we try to visit them at least once a year. We always come home so rested and refreshed. Walking the beach, you get that white sand between your toes and behind your ears. And when you walk to the water's edge, the sand packs down and the sea water takes over: the cool wetness, the smell, the salty taste reminds you how very much alive you are at that moment. And the bright sun makes the world seem brighter still: the beach, the ocean, the palm trees, the clear sky— all seem more colorful, more dazzling, more *alive*.

Even though we visit Florida regularly, it never becomes familiar to me; its mysteries appeal to my senses, dilating them. But that's true wherever I travel: I seem to see things more clearly, smell things more acutely, even feel things more finely when I'm on vacation or a visit. And that's the way that I'd invite readers to spend this fifth day of devotion. *Wherever you are,* try to see people and places as if for the first time. Let your senses dilate. When you experience the world anew, you can experience your *life* anew—and all healing entails some level of renewal.

If you think of yourself as a sojourner, you will never grow weary of the world. Some people grow accustomed to their sorrows and sicknesses, as if these were "part of the landscape of their lives." But the journey of healing—the path that you're on now, for the fifth day—leads down strange and delightful paths as yet unknown. So devote day 5 to emotional and spiritual "vacationing."

Take a day-trip if you can: in the Ozarks where we live, there are quaint hamlets with turn-of-the-century town squares and old antique shops. So go antiquing. Or, if you're like me, you'll go to one of the lakes or nature reserves.

Let the path of healing take you *off* the "beaten path." And if you can't take that trip physically, then read a travel book and imagine …

Wherever you spend day 5, do it as a sojourner …

When my family returns from a visit to Florida, we bring back souvenirs—and stories, like the time my brother-in-law John asked if I'd like to go mullet fishing with him. "Mullet fishing! Wow, sure," I said, even though I didn't know what a mullet was.

It was late afternoon when we packed up the car and headed to John's "secret" fishing hole. As we drove, he explained the rules. We weren't going to use rods and reels. Instead, my brother-in-law was going to wade chest-high into the water and cast a net. My job was to follow him into the water and carry the fish basket what would hold his catch.

"How utterly exotic and *ancient*," I thought to myself: "this casting of nets—we don't do *that* in Lake Springfield. They did that in the Sea of Galilee; and they do that here in Florida. But not in the Ozarks …"

With the skill of a native, John cast his net and hauled in fish. Carefully, so as not to hurt them, he removed the small fry and threw them back. Then he handed me the mullets that we'd be eating for supper that evening. Yes they were slimy, and some of them slipped out of my hands. But most made their way into the basket and, through it all, I was having a wonderfully wet time.

We had been fishing for about an hour and the basket was getting a bit heavy when I felt something bump against my leg. Foolishly at first, I was put off by the very notion that something would be so bold as to invade my space. But then I recalled the words of my father-in-law Bill: "The ocean is a dangerous place, Alvin, and, as a human being, you're out of your element. In the ocean, you're lower on the food-chain than you might think. Above all, be sure to drag your feet along the bottom when you walk. Sting Rays are bottom dwellers, and if you step on one its stinger could kill you." Whoa ...

"Hey, John," I said in a timid voice: "Something just bumped against my leg."

In a tone of utter matter-of-factness, my brother-in-law replied, "Oh it was likely a hammer-head shark just checking you out." For him, that was business as usual. But for me, I was in way too deep.

"I've had enough of mullet fishing—I'm out of here," was my reply. John laughed as I made my escape. I didn't walk on the water. I *ran*—and I must say that the Apostle Peter had nothing on me that afternoon as I fought my way out of the ocean!

That evening, we deep fried those fine Florida mullets and ate them with grandma's homemade hush puppies and coleslaw. And as we ate, two stories circulated of my hammer-head encounter. There was my version, where I narrowly escaped death. And there was John's version, where I let the unfamiliar defeat me. "You weren't in danger, not really," he said, smiling between bites.

He was right; my fear was misplaced, and I take Jeremiah 5.22 as my proof text:

> Should you not fear me? declares the LORD.... I made the sand a boundary for the sea, an everlasting barrier it cannot cross. The waves may roll, but they cannot prevail; they may roar, but they cannot cross it.

Indeed, the ocean waves may raise a mighty roar and we may stand in awe of their power—but their power is nothing compared to God's. Even the waves retreat, in obedience to their Creator.

Jeremiah is spot-on: the only righteous fear is fear of the LORD.

Still, sometimes we let the unfamiliar keep us from exploring the paths—or the depths—before us. Healing will always take us to places where anxieties war against hope. I could have trusted my brother-in-law John. I should have trusted him. Sometimes, when we're at a crossroads in our healing, we need to rely on people who have preceded us and have learned the lay of the land—or the ocean floor.

5. It's Your Turn to Reflect and Write.

"Wade in the water," goes the Negro spiritual: "Wade in the water, children." Part of the path is trust. If we fear and obey God—even as the ocean waves obey him—we'll be kept safe. So go out on day 5 and be a sojourner; take delight in the unfamiliar, and don't be afraid to out wading.

Throughout this fifth day of devotion, think of your healing path as an adventure. And practice relaxation. Journeying isn't always constant travel: at times, you need to stop and refresh.

When I'm stressed or overtired, sometimes I'll imagine myself by the waterside of a bright Florida beach, with the sand squishing between my toes. I'll breathe in the salt air and bend down to pick up a seashell that the tide has just thrown up on shore. I'll gaze at its pearl-like swirls of color, admiring God's handiwork in nature. And, as I imagine the scene, my breathing will slow and my muscles relax.

How about you? Can you write of a place that brings peace into your heart? Remember to give details: appeal to all five senses …

For your writing:

Day 6.
Follow the Red Letters

> Then Jacob awoke from his sleep and said,
> "Surely the Lord is in this place, and I did not
> know it." (Genesis 28.16)

If you were alive on November 22, 1963, I bet you
remember exactly where you were when you heard
that President Kennedy had been shot. Same with
January 28, 1986, when the Space Shuttle Challenger exploded upon takeoff. Same with September 11, 2001, when the mighty Twin Towers were
brought down by terrorists. These were transforming moments in our collective, national consciousness.

Fortunately, not all of our strongest memories are
of national disasters. Some are joyous, and some
belong to us individually. And so, on this sixth
day of your healing journey, I invite you to draw
strength from the moment when you became a
Christian—for, surely, the path you walk today was
established for you from that fateful day forward.

I remember the exact moment in time when I
received Christ as the Lord of my life, but let me

tell you about my grandfather's transforming moment.

My maternal grandfather, Mack Freeman, was a hard-working man and, after a week's worth of labor, he looked forward to his regular Sunday afternoon naps. And so, one Sunday afternoon, he laid himself down and fell asleep. What he didn't know was that the men of the local church had placed him on their "top ten list" of men to pray for. And they were meeting that Sunday afternoon at the church to pray.

During his nap, he dreamt a dream—a dream so real that, when he woke up, he responded. It may not have been as momentous as Jacob's dream; but, for my grandfather, it had all the markings of a message from the Lord. In his dream, he was trapped inside a cornucopia or horn-of-plenty, one of those basket-like decorations we've all seen at Thanksgiving that serves as a table centerpiece. He was trapped and the opening was on fire, so there was no way for him to get out as the other end tapered down to nothing.

"God," he said in his dream, "get me out of this and I will give my heart and life to you." He awoke in a state of agitation, much like Jacob: "Surely the Lord is in this place, and I did not know it."

At that moment, my grandfather could have said the same. He didn't know what to do; but he knew he needed to do something, so he walked to the church. He didn't expect anyone to be there at 2:30 in the afternoon, but as he approached he saw horses and buggies out in front. When he walked in, the men said, "Mack, we've been waiting on you as we've been praying for you."

That very day, Mack Freeman surrendered his life to the Lordship of Jesus Christ. And from that day until the day he died, when he went to be with his Lord, his life was filled with adventure and joy.

He shared that a man he worked with was a hard man, someone who lived fast and raw and without regard to man or goodness. God laid this man on my grandfather's heart and he began to pray with him. On one occasion he gave this man a Bible and told him that if he ever needed help, he should just follow the red letters and he would find all that he was looking for. Years went by. And when the man lay on his death bed, he told his wife that he had followed the red letters—and they had led him to Christ Jesus.

On this sixth day of your spiritual journey, you might consider my grandfather's advice. If ever there was a roadmap to spiritual health, it would lie in the red letters—the saving words of Jesus, as highlighted in the Bible. Nowadays, not all Bibles are "red letter" editions. But the words of our Lord will always stand out in Scripture.

6. It's Your Turn to Reflect and Write. Throughout this sixth day of devotion, reflect on the moment when Jesus entered your life. Write it down: preserve the moment for posterity.

Think about His words, marked in red, as the roadmap for your present spiritual journey. And fill the day with prayer—joyous prayer.

And now, to get the joy-juices flowing, think of yourself as a cheerleader for the Lord. Get out your imaginary pompoms and recite the following as if you were cheering your favorite team—the Lord's Faithful—on to victory. Don't be embarrassed: cheer it! Chant it! Sing it!

Take some time today TO PRAY!

P-R-A — Y-E-R!

P—Pause from the busyness of life!

R—Repent!

A—Acknowledge God!

Y—Yield unto the Lord!

E—Embark! (Do what He asks of you!)

R—Receive God's answer to your prayers!

For your writing:

Day 7.
"I saw the Light"

Congratulations! You have finished the first week of your devotional journey. Today, let me share with you some of my own youthful sojourning through the American Great Plains.

While serving in the United States Air Force, I was stationed in South Dakota. On weekends, my buddies and I would hop into my C-J 5 Jeep and we we'd go four-wheeling through South Dakota, Wyoming, and Montana.

We'd ride through the pristine landscape—it was breath-taking!—with no cares of life at all.

One day, somewhere near Billings, Montana, we came upon a herd of wild horses. They were fearless animals, especially the Stallion leader: a beautiful, strong horse. There were about twenty of them, and they allowed us to get very close—close enough that I could see their untrimmed manes and tails and the hair on their hoofs. Their hair flowed long and free, like the rest of their bodies.

As he grazed, the Stallion leader kept his eye on us, giving an occasional snort and paw of the ground.

We were no horse whisperers, so we knew we could come only so close to his family. And then, in a split second, they were off. The sun shone on their backs and I could see their muscles rippling as they broke into full gallop, as free as the morning air.

On another trip, we went to the Bad Lands to hunt for diamondbacks. It sounded like a great idea at the time, but such is youth. The cool northern air was refreshing, but by 9:00 a.m. the sun was beating down and the heat was rising, especially on the flat flint rocks that cover the Bad Lands. We were having a grand time until we turned over a large flat rock. And there, warming himself, was the biggest and loudest snake I had ever seen. We didn't know what to do: do we drop the rock and run, take a picture, or try to catch this coiled beauty?

Fortunately, we chose the wisest option: we turned tail and ran. But I'll never forget the rush of blood flowing through my veins as I came face to face with that very large, very dangerous snake.

One other weekend adventure that I'll never forget was traveling high into the Black Hills to hunt South Dakota mule deer. I've always enjoyed the outdoors and hunting; I knew the planning and patience and effort required for a successful hunt.

So we packed the Jeep and headed out in full expectation of success—not to mention of a good time. The three of us were young and full of spice and reckless abandon. We knew that the Black Hills were vast and that we could easily become separated. If that happened, our plan was to drive the lone road until we were each picked up. We had extra keys and the first one out would fire up the Jeep and drive back and forth until the other two came out onto the road.

I hunted all day, though, truth be told, I found the scenery so enthralling that I'd often just sit down on a rock and gaze about me, quietly blending into the woods. A light snow began falling around 2:00 p.m.—which is a hunter's delight, since tracking becomes easier. By 3:00 p.m., the snow was becoming wet and heavy and the temperature was falling sharply. As I was scanning the woods before me, I thought I heard someone walking up the trail. I figured it was one of my hunting buddies, but as I turned to look, I saw the most magnificent mule deer I had ever laid eyes on. Sensing something amiss, he turned and trotted away. I began tracking it. The snow was still increasing and the wind rising while the sun was falling in the west. It was now after 4:00 pm. And it suddenly came to me that, once the sun had set, the darkness would arrive that gave this place its ominous name, the Black Hills. At first, a wave of panic washed over me; but then my survival training kicked in.

I had decisions to make. If I tracked this animal and managed to shoot it, then what? Was I willing to spend the night protecting my meal from the wild? Without help, I certainly could not field-dress it and drag it out to the road, as it was well in excess of 200 pounds.

Fortunately again, that inner voice of wisdom won out: "Here in the Hills, people live about 50-60 miles apart. Don't expect help to arrive. You had better find your way out of this beautiful land back to civilization." Once again, a wave of panic hit me and my walking pace sped up, along with my heart rate. It didn't take long to realize that I had lost the landmarks I had so carefully picked to guide me back.

I was lost, indeed.

Knowing total darkness was mere moments away, I breathed a prayer: "Lord, I am Lost. I don't know where the road is. I don't know where my buddies are. And I really, really do not want to spend the night out here." At that instant I came into a clearing and, off in the far distance, I saw headlights. I couldn't hear the vehicle, but I saw headlights. And I knew that, where there were headlights, there would be a road back home. I checked the stars to confirm my bearings and headed toward the lights.

Two and a half hours later, weary, wet, and hungry—and very relieved—I stumbled out of the woods and onto the dirt road. And then, an hour later still, I heard the familiar motor of a Jeep coming towards me.

"I once was lost but now am found": that's the gospel life-message that pressed itself upon me at that moment, though I tried to cover up my feelings with a bit of USAF bravado: "Where have you guys been?" I said as I climbed in. "I've been here waiting on you—oh, and turn up the heater." Needless to say, they weren't buying what I was selling and my buddies never let me live down the weekend I got lost in the Black Hills of South Dakota.

It's often around this time—not quite mid-way on your path of healing—that feelings of lost-ness can assault you: have you gone so far out that you can't find your way back? Once doubt sets in, other emotions follow: panic can hit, and panic brings confusion, fear, despair. But remember: you have resources! Let the Bible be your textbook in survival training. And stay with the plan: pray, keep walking, and look for that flicker of light in the distance.

7. It's Your Turn to Reflect and Write. Through-out this seventh day of devotion, reflect on those moments when you "saw the light" and God revealed the path He made *just for you*. Though we may lead ourselves astray, God sends us Jesus—the "light of the world" (John 9.5)—to guide and pro-tect us.

Here on this seventh day, you might want to sit a spell, just as I did those many years back while out hunting in the Black Hills. Look at all that sur-rounds you. Take time to take it all in and admire it all: the beauty of God's creation, of friends and family, of the simple pleasures of life. Then reflect on the healing path that you've been walking these past seven days. How far have you come? Don't fuss at yourself if you're not as far along as you'd wished; instead, rejoice in the progress you've made! And then look forward: look for the light, that distant flickering light, which marks your goal and destination. See it in your mind's eye; give yourself fully to its guidance.

And repeat, throughout the day, "I am a child of the Light that guides me."

For your writing:

Day 8.
"Ma, I *Told* You ...!"

Therefore I … do not cease to give thanks for
you, making mention of you in my prayers:
that the God of our Lord Jesus Christ … may
give to you the spirit of wisdom and revelation in the knowledge of Him, the eyes of
your understanding being enlightened; that
you may know what is the hope of His calling,
what are the riches of the glory of His inheritance in the saints … (Ephesians 1.15-18)

"Never judge a book by its cover." We've all heard
that saying, but how often do we fall into that old,
bad habit? It's especially good advice when meeting people: we should never judge others by their
outward "cover"—whether it's their clothing or
appearance or mannerisms or the color of their
skin or whatever. Because it isn't always the way it
seems.

There was a pastor of a fairly large church. To
accommodate its growing membership, the
elders had approved plans for an extension onto
the church; so the members went to work, rolling up their sleeves. And the work proceeded
apace. But then, like so many projects in life, the
church's optimism had out-stripped its budget:

an additional $20,000 was needed to complete the building. So the pastor appealed to the church to borrow the money. The pastor made the appeal publicly and the congregation began praying.

The next week, an older man and his wife walked into the church. They were fairly new to the church and not everyone knew them by face or name. In appearance, they were simple folk—"dirt farmers," as I've heard city folk say, derisively. His coveralls were worn, while her smock-style work dress was plain and obviously hand-sewn. They stopped by the secretary's office and asked to see the pastor. "Wait here, please," responded the secretary: "I'll go tell the pastor you're wanting to see him. And what are your names again, please?…"

"An older couple wants to visit with you, pastor," said the secretary: "I'm not sure about these folks …"

By the looks of it, they had come asking for help: so the secretary assumed—and, with the church in need of money—it seemed a bad time to come asking …

The pastor came out and greeted them, asking how he or the church could help them. "Well," said the older gentleman, "we heard that the church needs some money. And we'd like to help in this matter." That said, the pastor immediately cleared his calendar of appointments and ushered them into his study. Seated across from the pastor's desk, the man leaned forward and said, "Now, we understand the need is $20,000."

"Yes it is," said the pastor.

"Well, we want to loan the church the $20,000."

Out of the lady's oversized pocket came a large glass jar filled to overflowing with twenties, fifties, and one hundred dollar bills. Staring at the fruit jar holding all that money, the pastor felt his heart skip a beat. The jar was opened, the money dumped out onto the pastor's desk, and the counting began.

"That's $19,995," the pastor declared, triumphantly: "Wow! Just $5.00 short of our goal. Thanks so much!" But the man looked at his wife and said, frowning, "Let's count it again." And again they counted it and again it came to $19,995. So the pastor reached into his pocket, pulled out his wallet, and took out a five dollar bill to add to the piles.

For a moment, the three of them just sat staring at the piles of money on the pastor's desk. It was the older man who broke the silence. Turning to his wife, he said, "Ma, *I told you*, you brought *the wrong jar!*"

I began this eighth day's devotion with verses from Paul's letter to the Ephesians. When Paul writes of "the riches of the glory of His inheritance in the saints," he challenges us to understand each word in its right spiritual context. Clearly the older couple had "riches" in abundance, but their true wealth was not stored up in old fruit jars: they were content to live simple lives while storing up their riches in Heaven, where they would enjoy "the glory of His inheritance in the saints."

This devotion has several messages, though two stand out to me. The first one I've already stated: when it comes to your fellow Christians, you can't judge what's *inside* from what's *outside*, on the mere surface. We should try harder to know the people around us—to know them not superficially by name and occupation but to know them deeply, personally. Because we can't ask for kindness or respect *from* others until we give kindness and respect *to* others.

The second message is somewhat subtler: as the older couple teaches us, there's richness in simplicity. One of the challenges we face in our healing journey is deciding what to take with us—in effect, to decide *what truly matters.* As a rule, we carry too much baggage. But when we simplify our lives, we reduce our worries and distractions. We have more time—more "riches" —to lavish on our church family, our own family, and on ourselves.

Let me change metaphors. In the old days of hot air balloon travel, balloonists hung sandbags over the side of the gondola; these sandbags served as ballast, helping the balloonist travel at a safe height. But if the balloonist began losing altitude—or simply wanted to soar—he'd jettison some bags. On this eighth day of your healing journey, think of yourself as a balloonist: in order to soar higher and swifter toward your goal, try lightening your load.

8. It's Your Turn to Reflect and Write. Throughout this eighth day of devotion, reflect on the "riches of the glory" that come from living a simpler, Spirit-filled life.

You might consider making two lists, the first of "things that matter" in your healing journey, the second of worries and concerns that are weighing you down—that you can do without. What ballast or baggage can you throw overboard, lightening your load?

For your writing:

Day 9.
The 3,000 Hit Club

Roberto Clemente remains one of the all-time greatest baseball players in major league history. By 1972, he had become the consummate ball-player. A twelve-time All Star with the Pittsburgh Pirates, he had won four batting titles, the National League Most Valuable Player Award, and a World Series Most Valuable Player Award. He had "won it all," and with his legacy secured, he could just play the game for the fun of it.

It was September 29, 1972—the last day of the regular season—and Clemente had chalked up 2,999 career hits. Only seven players before him had reached 3,000 and here he was, sitting at 2,999. And yet, on that last game of the season, only one hit shy of baseball history, Roberto was not going to play.

Before the game started, Bob Prince, the broadcaster and voice of the Pirates, noticed that Clemente's name was not penciled in the lineup. So he left the broadcasting booth and walked down to the field, where he asked Clemente why—why wasn't he in the lineup to make history?

Clemente told Prince, "It's good for marketing if I wait until next season to get my 3,000th career hit. It will help season ticket sales."

Prince told Roberto, "You never know what's going to happen, today or tomorrow." Clemente thought about it and decided to play in this final game—a home game at Three Rivers Stadium.

In the fourth inning, he smacked a double off of Mets pitcher, Jon Matlack. Standing on second base, he tipped his cap to the cheers of the crowd—and to the delight of the broadcaster. On that day in that game, Roberto Clemente became the eighth player in MLB history to record 3,000 hits.

Three months later, on December 31, 1972, Clemente boarded a plane to Nicaragua to deliver food and medicine to earthquake victims. His DC-7 crashed into the Atlantic Ocean. In one tragic moment, Roberto Clemente, aged thirty-eight, was gone.

Before the accident, he was quoted as saying, "Anytime you have an opportunity to make things better and you don't, then you're just wasting your time on earth."

Clemente was fortunate to have had Prince for a friend. And the advice Prince gave could easily have come from the letter of James:

> Come now, you who say, "Today or tomorrow we will go to such and such a city, spend a year there, buy and sell, and make a profit"; whereas you do not know what will happen tomorrow. For what is your life? It is even a vapor that appears for a little time and then vanishes away. Instead you ought to say, "If the Lord wills, we shall live and do this or that." (4.13-16)

As usual, there is more than one lesson to a story. The first is to make every day count, because "you do not know what will happen tomorrow." The second is to make God's will, and not your own, the focus of your intentions and desires. When I was younger, the Scriptural phrase, "God willing" ended many an expression of hope or intention; nowadays, not so much. As a community, we should get back in the habit of making God's will the foundation for our choices and actions.

9. It's Your Turn to Reflect and Write. Throughout this ninth day of devotion, reflect on the preciousness of the present moment, in full awareness that "you do not know what will happen tomorrow."

And here's a writing exercise. Imagine that this is your last day on earth and that you're making a to-do list of everything you need to accomplish on this fateful final day. What do you need to "make right"? Does anyone need forgiving? Do *you* need forgiving? We're often stingy with the words, "I love you." Who on your list needs to hear these words?

When you're done writing out your final day's to-do list, make that same list your to-do list *today*—and tomorrow, and the next day, and the next. Remember that *every* day needs to be lived as if it were your last on earth. For if you live in that way, you'll live in peace with God, your neighbor, and yourself.

For your writing:

Day 10.
Seeing the Son in the Sun

> For I know the thoughts that I think toward
> you, says the Lord,… to give you a future and a
> hope. (Jeremiah 29.11)

It was a glorious Sunday afternoon. And on this
beautiful Lord's Day, I had been invited to speak
at a country church. I was still in Bible College,
so any invitation to any place was welcome. As a
student, I had more questions than answers, but
I was willing to approach the pulpit and looked
forward to having ears to speak to that were willing
to listen.

I arrived early and sat in my car in the church
parking lot, fumbling through my message notes. I
was excited and nervous at the same time. To this
day, I still get preacher's butterflies in the pit of
my stomach. But I don't mind them, much: they
remind me that I still care and they keep me on my
toes, always preparing.

The topic for the evening was "God's Revealed
Glory." So I had been praying, asking God to reveal
His glory to me in some tangible way. I didn't want
to speak of God's glory, merely: I wanted to make

it manifest, *to do it* by some miraculous healing of the sick, by making the blind see, by turning something into something else …

You get the picture. Remember, I was a student at the time.

And that afternoon, while sitting nervously in a small country church parking lot, God taught me an unforgettable lesson.

I heard His voice speaking to me. If I ever hear His voice audibly I'm planning on recording it, so others can hear it, too. But the voice I heard came from within my spirit man. I've come to recognize that soft, still voice and to rely on it throughout my years of ministry.

When His voice spoke to me, the late afternoon was turning to dusk. The sun was falling below the horizon, though a red half-circle remained at eye level and visible through my windshield. Shadows were beginning to fall around me and darkness was beginning to fill the parking lot. And as I sat there, His voice to me said:

Look at the sun. At high noon, no one can look directly into the sun's full glory. No one can gaze into the sun's full flame. *So it is with Me!* When you look to me you will see the reflection of my good-

ness and my glory. You will see the smile of a new-
born baby, and the shadows will fall behind you.

I remember His words to this day. Yes, God
revealed His glory to me in that church parking
lot—and he gave me my sermon message for that
evening, as well.

10. It's Your Turn to Reflect and Write. Throughout this tenth day of devotion, reflect on the soft, still voice of God as He speaks within. What words has He spoken to you? Have you ever written them down? Have you ever shared them with others?

Remember that God is your companion throughout this journey of healing. If you ask, He will answer. But be aware that the external noises of life—not to mention the incessant chatter going on inside our heads—can drown out that soft, still voice. So take time during this tenth day to sit quietly, still your mind, and talk to God.

And then *listen*. Do this several times throughout the day, but especially during the rising and setting sun. At noon its brightness is blinding, but at dawn and dusk you will "see the reflection" of His goodness and His glory, "and the shadows will fall behind you."

For your writing:

Day 11.
Chippie's Bad Day

Poor Chippie: he never knew what hit him.

One minute he was peacefully perched inside his bird cage, and the next he was sucked in, drowned under, scrubbed up, rolled over, and almost blown to smithereens!

Chippie's bad day began when his owner decided to vacuum out his bird cage. She stuck the hose attachment inside the cage, and all the seed husks and dried Chippie-poo disappeared down the long, grey snake with a magical little "poof!" sound now and then. And that's when the ringing telephone distracted her.

When she returned, her parakeet was gone!

In a panic, she opened the vacuum canister and tore open the bag inside. And, sure enough, there was Chippie, buried among the dust bunnies and seed husks, stunned but alive. He blinked at her once, but all in all, he didn't seem inclined to move from his burrow.

He was covered with dirt, dust, dog hairs, pulverized seed husks, and who knows what else. In a second panic she reached in, wrapped her fingers around the little bird body, and lifted him out of the vacuum bag. Then she ran down the hall to the bathroom where she turned on both water taps full-blast, stuck him under the faucet, and began pulling out of his feathers as much of the dirt and debris that would dislodge under the water's torrent.

Though determined that not a speck of filth would remain on Chippie, she felt his little legs struggling to push against her fingers. So she removed him from under the downpour. Her poor bird looked more like a soaked, shivering, semi-drowned rat than a parakeet.

So, she leapt into action and did what any compassionate bird owner would do. She grabbed her jet pro-speed ceramic double-power flash-blow dryer and cranked it up.

Chippie never knew what hit him.

But when he finally came to his senses, he wriggled out of her grasp, flew up, and perched indignantly on the shower rod, where he sat with his feathers ruffled mightily around him and one glaring eye fixed on her for what seemed a very long time.

It took some time to coax him down from the shower rod and back into his freshly cleaned cage. It took even longer for his head feathers—which bristled like an enraged cockatoo's—to relax back into place.

A friend called a few days later to ask how Chippie was coming along.

"Well," the owner said, "he looks no worse for wear, really, but I can't get him to sing and talk like he used to. He just sits on his perch and glares at me!"

Well, I imagine he would! Getting sucked in, drowned under, scrubbed up, and blown over, he'd had enough to render the best talkers speechless and to take the song from the stoutest of hearts.

Haven't we all had those days when everything that could go wrong did go wrong? And when we do, don't we feel as if we're the only person who has ever been through so much for so little gain?

Now consider the story of Job. The old epithet, "the patience of Job," is more than an age-old phrase— he really was long-suffering and he really didn't lose his faith, even though he was put through every loss imaginable to see if he would turn away from God. Even his health was taken from him, and yet he would not curse God.

But you'd be missing the point if you thought that patient Job, faithful Job, was "silent, smiling Job" through it all. By no means. He talked, he questioned, he agonized over his situation; he tried every way he could to figure out why all this was happening to him. You can hear the pain in Job's lament:

> "Why is light given to a man whose way is hidden, And whom God has hedged in? For my sighing comes before I eat, And my groanings pour out like water. For the thing I greatly feared has come upon me, And what I dreaded has happened to me. I am not at ease, nor am I quiet; I have no rest, for trouble comes." (Job 3.23-26)

We know that life's trials sometimes cloud our paths. We want to walk with the Lord, but His ways seem "hidden" at times. And there's something worse than a "path" seemingly hidden; it's when God Himself—the beacon that had guided Job on his life's path—feels hidden from us, as well. Here's what Job has to say:

"Look, I go forward, but He is not there, And backward, but I cannot perceive Him; When He works on the left hand, I cannot behold Him; When He turns to the right hand, I cannot see Him.But He knows the way that I take; When He has tested me, I shall come forth as gold. (Job 23.8-10)

So often, when we are in our deepest worry or fear—that is, when we most need to feel God's presence—we search frantically for His calming assurance. But we should know that God is always with us and watching over us, even if we're unaware of Him. As Job declares, "He knows the way that I take."

On this eleventh day of your journey, remember Job!

When you seem to have lost direction, trust in God to keep you on the path. And *don't* be like that sullen parakeet, Chippie, that shuts up in anger. Just like Job, *let your feelings out*. If you feel *de*-pressed, take time *to ex*-press yourself in some creative way.

I remember one cold Missouri morning when I was attending a neighbor's funeral. We had arrived at the graveside service and I was sitting in my car with the motor and heater running for a while longer. I was thinking about how bad this day was shaping up to be. Then I thought to take out a piece of paper and write down my feelings of the moment. This is what I penned:

Life

Life is tough at times
even on the straight and narrow way.

Life is short
yet the walk is long.

Remember now thy Creator
in the days of thy strength and glory.

Hold your head up high and smile—
Face into the sun and see the dawn of life's
new day.

Look
full of faith and assurance in the face of God:
He sees and cares.

Be strong in trust and in confidence of
His Sweet Spirit,
trusting in His strong arms to bring you
through.

When at last the warrior's sword is laid to
rest upon the grassy knoll,
Then sings my soul,
sweet victory!

For now in Christ
I've won at last
Eternal Life.

I've won at last
Eternal life.

11. It's Your Turn to Reflect and Write. Throughout this eleventh day of devotion, remind yourself that God will be faithful to you if you're faithful to Him. He will keep you on the path of healing, even when you feel directionless. Repeat this throughout the day: "God will keep me on the path of healing."

Chances are that your dis-ease—of whatever sort, be it of body, mind, or spirit—has "put you through the wringer," like that poor parakeet (or even like Job). But don't let the hurt or anger fester inside! Let it out—and let it go.

Give your symptoms a "piece of your mind," *and then give them to God* for His disposal. You'll feel better if you do.

And then, if you feel inspired, write some words of praise.

For your writing:

Day 12.
Keep Knocking!

"So I say to you, ask, and it will be given to you; seek, and you will find; knock, and it will be opened to you. For everyone who asks receives, and he who seeks finds, and to him who knocks it will be opened." (Luke 11.9-10)

Life is filled with so many questions. Why am I here? What is my purpose? What about the future, my tomorrows?

There are times when we do not have the answers to simple yet profound questions of life (like why do black cows that eat green grass produce white milk and yellow butter?). But, as we reflect over a given moment, a day, a month, a year, or a lifetime, we see the hand of a gracious God leading our steps.

I come from a large Ozarks family, a family that loves home and hearth, country, and God. I guess we're the all-American apple pie, flag-waving bunch you often hear about. And we boys were ready to do our duty when called.

My older brothers and I grew up in a turbulent era in our nation's history. It was 1970, the Vietnam War was raging, and the government had instituted a lottery draft. Males born between 1944 and 1950 had to register and a random selection was made by birthdate. The first 195 birthdates were called to service in the order they were drawn by lottery: the earlier your number (that is, your birthdate) was drawn, the sooner you were called to serve. Well, my older twin brothers, Leslie Dean and Weslie Gene, shared a birthdate. (That's no surprise.) And when the lottery was held, their number was fairly high on the list, so both of them were drafted.

Our grandmother was a lady of grace and beauty, but she was also a prayer warrior and she worried over the prospect of having not one, but two of her grandchildren slogging through Vietnamese rice paddies. She knew how to invade the darkness and knock on Heaven's door. Our Godly grandmother believed in Asking, Seeking, and Knocking in prayer. So when word came that Leslie and Weslie both had been drafted, Grandma Bee went to her prayer closet. She had a little talk with Heaven. I don't know what she prayed, but I do know she was knock- knock- knocking on Heaven's door.

The day came for our brothers to board the bus from Springfield to the Selective Service Station in Kansas City. The government had leased the entire bus and every seat was taken. Leslie Dean and Weslie Gene were both seated on this bus.

Just before the door closed, a soldier got on, walked over to my brother sitting in the front of the bus, tapped him on the shoulder, and said, "You get off this bus." Then he walked to the back of the bus where my other brother was seated, tapped him on the shoulder, and said, "You get off this bus."

Once outside the bus, the soldier said to both brothers together, "We'll call you if and when we need you. Just go home and wait." That call never came.

As an Air Force man myself whose daughter served in the U.S. Army in Iraq, I'd expect that my brothers would have served honorably, had they been called. But God—and my grandmother —had other plans for them.

The story of my grandmother is like the parable of the friend at midnight, whose persistence wins out in the end:

And He said to them, "Which of you shall have a friend, and go to him at midnight and say to him, 'Friend, lend me three loaves; for a friend of mine has come to me on his journey, and I have nothing to set before him'; and he will answer from within and say, 'Do not trouble me; the door is now shut, and my children are with me in bed; I cannot rise and give to you'? I say to you, though he will not rise and give to him because he is his friend, yet because of his persistence he will rise and give him as many as he needs." (Luke 11.5-8)

Prayer that's intermittent or lukewarm won't do the trick. Persistence is the key. Keep knocking on Heaven's door. God's timing and manner of answering often comes just in time.

12. It's Your Turn to Reflect and Write. Throughout this twelfth day of devotion, reflect on the manner of your praying. Is your praying persistent? Or is it intermittent, lukewarm?

Whatever you need most on this twelfth day, be tireless in your Seeking, Asking, and Knocking. And don't be selfish: your coworkers, friends, and family have need of your prayers, too.

For your writing:

Day 13.
Watch Your Words

"Do you not yet understand that whatever enters the mouth goes into the stomach and is eliminated? But those things which proceed out of the mouth come from the heart, and they defile a man." (Matthew 15.17-18)

In our treatment of other people, there's no such thing as a "mere word." Our words leave their marks on others, because words *do* things to others. While kind words calm and sooth, harsh words act like sandpaper, leaving scratch marks on people's emotions.

Words can wound us: we've all been cut by another's criticism—words can be sharp as knives. But words can also heal us: think of the release that comes from such words as "I love you," or "I'm sorry, forgive me." Our emotions are so thoroughly intertwined with language that the very utterance of some words has its effect on our pulses: "love," "death," "joy," "grief," "fear," "hope." Words like these invoke whole worlds of emotion.

So remember that you're never just *speaking,* you're also *doing* by means of the words you speak. And remember that you're going be judged by the words you speak and by their effects.

I recall a story I heard while in Seminary that is so to the point.

There was a man who felt caught in the rat race of life. Every time he'd seem to pull up even or get a nose ahead, along would come a faster rat. So he retreated from the rat race altogether and decided to join a monastery. It so happens that the monastic order he chose imposed three vows on its brethren: chastity, poverty—and silence.

The rules were simple and straightforward. Once you entered you were not allowed to speak: all you could do was pray, meditate, write, and carry out the responsibilities of monastic life. There was, however, a rule that allowed two words to be spoken every five years. "*This is perfect!*" the man thought to himself: "*No stress, no fuss, no one troubling me with their problems—this is what I've been looking for.*" So he took his vows and walked through the monastery's gates, looking forward to a life of silent tranquility.

The first few years were serene, but as the fifth year approached the man thought hard about which two words he would say. He had to choose his words carefully. So the fifth anniversary of his vows arrived and he spoke: "Bad food."

The years came and went and he was approaching the tenth anniversary of his vows, when he would be allowed to speak two more words. Again he chose his words carefully: "Hard bed."

The man found himself closing in on the fifteenth anniversary of his vows, which caused him to do a lot of hard thinking. He had two more words to speak, and again he chose his words carefully: "I quit."

With that the Father Superior couldn't stand it anymore and blasted out, "Well I'm not surprised. You've done nothing but complain ever since you got here."

13. It's Your Turn to Reflect and Write. Through-out this thirteenth day of devotion, listen carefully to the words people speak and to the effect they have on others. Are there people in your life whose conversation is littered with complaints? Are your friends addicted to gossip? Can you see the effects of their words as they claw, scratch, and bite at the world?

Throughout this day, watch your own words, too. You've heard of "friendly fire," when ordinance aimed at an enemy hits one's fellows. Even if unin-tentional, a thoughtless word can harm a friend. In this respect, it's the end results that matter, so don't let your words become "friendly fire" or cause "collateral damage."

Make sure that your words to others are kind and encouraging. And make sure that your words to yourself—for we *do* speak to ourselves throughout the day—are kind and encouraging, too. Remem-ber that affirmation is a powerful instrument in healing, and that affirmation begins with words. Again and again, say to yourself, "With God's help, *I will heal*," and let your words guide your inten-tions. Let your words stimulate your willpower.

And remember, you have to invite God into your life: *that's the best use of your words,* in my opinion.

For your writing:

This is a reminder to me
to use words for myself
as well as others. I
tend to be a non-sharer
(which hasn't been good for me)
I've learned over the
years that not sharing good
or bad can have a neg. impact
on everyone b/c it leaves so
much to wonder about. Are
they happy w/my work, do they
value me, am I doing the
right thing.... and while all
of that is important it
reminded me most to open up
to God b/c He knows what my fears

Day 14.
The Demon-Possessed Chicken

Trust in the Lord with all your heart,
And lean not on your own understanding;
In all your ways acknowledge Him,
And He shall direct your paths.

Do not be wise in your own eyes; fear the Lord
and depart from evil.
It will be health to your flesh,
And strength to your bones.
(Proverbs 3.5-8)

Having finished our second week of devotional
journeying together, I'd like to tell a humorous
story (at my expense, I might add), though one
with a serious theme.

I was blessed with wonderful grandparents. In
fact, I could not have asked for a better family.
Their roots go back to the Arkansas hills where
the Freemans, my mother's parents, lived. I would
say I was five (or nearing six at most) when I took
my first trip deep into the Arkansas back woods.
Compared to Springfield, Missouri, it appeared to
me to be the end of the earth. Now I have nothing
against Arkansas. My little sister is currently min-

+ insecurities are anyway. Be humble.

istering there. I did, however, ruffle her feathers with a remark about Arkansas building a larger zoo than the San Diego and St. Louis zoos put together. I told her that they were just going to fence the whole state in. (Sorry, Razorback fans: nothing personal.)

At any rate, I'll never forget the day my parents took us to visit some relations who lived on a farm back in the hills. Being all of five years old, I wasn't too concerned about the occasion, whether it was a family reunion or just a visit. What I do remember is that for supper we were going to have chicken.

Our relations were poor and when they wanted chicken they didn't go to the store or to Colonel Sanders's house, they went to the chicken coop. And they didn't call them chickens: they called them fryers, 'cause that's what happened to them.

That afternoon, I went with an older cousin down to the chicken coop. Those chickens got stirred up, like they knew what was about to happen. I stayed close behind the big legs of my relative as he caught one. To a five-year-old boy, those were some mean chickens, running around and making all kinds of noises. To this day, I imagine those Arkansas chickens were demon-possessed.

We took that fryer and went out to a stump. Feathers were flying, mad chickens were running all around, and my relation held this chicken by the throat, trying to lay it down on that stump. I was about to find out why that chicken didn't want to lie down on that stump. With one swift swoop, down comes my cousin's axe and off goes the chicken's head. Blood flew everywhere. And then I saw something I had never seen before: the chicken began running around, headless. In fact, this headless demonic chicken came running straight at me, or so I thought. So I began to running and crying at the same time.

"That ole chicken can't hurt you, boy," said my cousin, laughing: "It's dead."

The problem, as I saw it, was that the chicken *didn't know* it was dead; its head was gone, but its body was running. But then, just in the nick of time, just before this headless chicken caught me and sank its demon claws into my flesh, it fell over, kicked its feet a few times, and just chickened out.

That night at supper when the chicken plate was passed around, I took my time looking over each piece, expecting any moment that the plate would come to life and start chasing me all over again. I survived my ordeal. But even to this day, whenever we have chicken for dinner, I remember that encounter in the back woods of Arkansas.

Is there a message in this story? *I think there is.*

Many times the sorrowful or worrisome things in our past seem never to die. Or they manage to come back to life, even after they're over and done with.

I've heard it said that FEAR is FALSE EVIDENCE APPEARING REAL. Don't let ghosts of the past haunt you. Let the past be the past—and pass the chicken, please …

14. It's Your Turn to Reflect and Write. Throughout this fourteenth day of devotion, I invite you to put your demons to rest, to bury the past, to be done with old wounds and sorrows. We've spent the past two weeks together. Now let's stop to survey where we've come from and the distance we've traveled. Remember: None of it means a thing if we let sorrows of the past come back to life and possess us still.

So I want you to pretend with me that you're putting each old habit, each bad memory, each symptom and each sorrow into a paper bag. Then tie each bag to a helium balloon. And then let go of each balloon. Let it float away from you: disinterested and unattached, watch it float up and away from you, disappearing into the distance, forever.

For your writing:

Day 15.
"Life Is Just a Minute"

The Reverend Benjamin Elijah Mays (1894-1984) was an African American civil rights leader, a university president, and a Baptist minister. He is most famous for giving the benediction at the close of the March on Washington in 1963, but I hold him most fondly for a little poem that he wrote, titled "Life is Just a Minute":

> Life is just a minute—only sixty seconds in it.
> Forced upon you—can't refuse it.
> Didn't seek it—didn't choose it.
> But it's up to you to use it.
> You must suffer if you lose it.
> Give an account if you abuse it.
> Just a tiny, little minute,
> But eternity is in it!

I could quote verse upon verse of Scripture echoed in this little poem, but the passage that weighs heavy on my heart is Revelation 1.3: "Blessed *is* he who reads and those who hear the words of this prophecy, and keeps those things which are written in it; for the time *is* near."

Indeed, I believe with all my heart that the time *is* near. And that's why, on this fifteenth day of devotion, I want to remind you that the journey of your life is a journey *in* time and *through* time, whose ultimate destination is *eternity*.

We are responsible for "redeeming the time," as Paul writes in Ephesians 5.16. But the Reverend Mays's poem, echoing Revelation and Ephesians—and the whole of Scripture, in fact—reminds us of time's double aspect. There's our paltry human time, and then there's God's time—or, rather, God's timelessness. As Psalm 90.1-6 declares,

> Lord, You have been our dwelling place in all
> generations.
> Before the mountains were brought forth,
> Or ever You had formed the earth and the
> world,
> Even from everlasting to everlasting, You are
> God.
>
> You turn man to destruction,
> And say, "Return, O children of men."
> For a thousand years in Your sight
> Are like yesterday when it is past,
> And like a watch in the night.
> You carry them away like a flood;

They are like a sleep.
In the morning they are like grass which grows
up:
In the morning it flourishes and grows up;
In the evening it is cut down and withers.

And so should we live our lives—that is, use the
time allotted to us—with eternity constantly in
mind. For worldly time *is situated within* God's
eternity: that, indeed, is the message of Mays's
sweet little poem.

15. It's Your Turn to Reflect and Write. Throughout this fifteenth day of devotion, I'd like you to practice living "with eternity in mind." I have another old poem to quote on this subject, though the author is anonymous. Titled "Take Time," it's been copied in sermon notebooks, recorded in diaries, and printed for framing. It's the sort of "wisdom poem" that was popular during the lives of our grandparents, and I suspect that old framed copies still survive in dusty attics. Needless to say, its advice holds for us still, in these latter days:

Take time to think—
    It is the source of all power.
Take time to read—
    It is the foundation of all wisdom.
Take time to play—
    It is the source of perpetual youth.
Take time to be quiet—
    It is the opportunity to seek God.
Take time to be aware—
    It is the opportunity to help others.
Take time to love and be loved—
    It is God's greatest gift.
Take time to laugh—
    It is the music of the soul.
Take time to be friendly—
    It is the road to happiness.

Take time to dream—
   It is what the future is made of.
Take time to pray—
   It is the greatest power on earth.
Take time to give—
   It is too short a day to be selfish.
Take time to work—
   It is the price of success.

Throughout the day, "take time" to do the things mentioned above. And keep in mind that, whatever you do today, "eternity" is *already* "in it."

For your writing:

There are many things that spoke to
me this day. 1: recognize that everything
(I am reminded)
within my life is <u>His</u> timing, not my own.
2: 'Redeeming the time', choose what im
doing (redeeming) wisely

    + I love the sentence about God
being timeless!"

    # Worldly time is within God's eternity
in His grasp'
3: Taking time for me is not selfish, it is
    commanded. I should be mindful of
    the <u>TIME</u> HE has allowed me +
    be fruitful in it.

Day 16.
Choices and Promises

"Before I formed you in the womb I knew you."
(Jeremiah 1.5)

With lab tests in hand, the obstetrician entered the examination room and closed the door behind him. This should have been a routine exam for the pregnant Anna Marie. But she hadn't been feeling well for several weeks, so the somber look on the doctor's face seemed ominous.

Seating himself by the examination table, he gave the bad news: "Anna, there are complications to your pregnancy that are endangering your life. You've developed an infection whose toxins have stressed the functioning of your liver, kidneys, and heart. As your doctor, I would advise you to terminate this pregnancy. You can always have another child, but your children only have one mother. Go home and think it over, talk it over, then tell me what you want to do. I'm sorry."

With a forced half-smile and a handshake, the physician left to see his next patient, leaving her with the heaviest of burdens. *What was she to do?*

This young mother of two faced the decision of her life. She could save the baby and lose her own life. She could save her own life and lose the baby. It was a life-and-death decision of the sort she had never dreamed of facing. It would test the strength of her faith.

Of course her husband and family consoled and advised her. And of course she prayed—hard. She prayed and prayed until God spoke to her heart in that still, small voice that she recognized as His alone: "*I am going to use your baby for my service.*"

With the support of her husband and family, Anna Marie made her decision and phoned the doctor, telling him that she was going to have her baby. She had based her decision not on medical data, not on rational argument, but on the deep assurance God had planted within her heart.

It was a difficult pregnancy, but she had good medical care, the strong support of family and friends, and a whole lot of praying on her side. And so, on January 14, 1952, Anna Marie gave birth to a little boy. In fact, he was the last baby born in the old St. John's Hospital in Springfield, Missouri. A newer, more modern facility was being readied for occupancy and this old one was being shut down.

In case you're interested, Anna Marie named her baby Alvin G. Blackard, Jr. Yes, that baby was me. And, yes, I have been a minister of His Grace for thirty-plus years. God was faithful to the promise He made to my mother, and my mother stood firm in her faith in God. My dear Anna Marie has only recently gone to be with the Lord, and I cherish the riches that she brought to my life, knowing full well that I owe my life—literally—to her courage and her trust in the Lord.

How could I not take that courage, that trust, as my life-model? Often when I face a tough decision, I imagine myself in that hospital room in old St. John's together with the doctor and my mother. Then I work toward a decision worthy of my mother's courage and the Lord's approval.

16. It's Your Turn to Reflect and Write. Throughout this sixteenth day of devotion, I invite you to remember and celebrate the lives of those who came before you (or with you) and served as role models: give thanks for their instruction-by-example. There are likely many such role models—more than you might imagine. I hope that parents, grandparents, siblings, and other relatives make it on that list. I hope that a wife or a husband—and maybe a pastor or two!—will make it on that list, as well. But there will be others on the list: a neighbor, a teacher, a roommate or friend, maybe a mere acquaintance whose actions and character caught your attention one day and taught you something about life.

And once you think of some people really special, maybe—assuming they're alive and you have their postal address, email, or Facebook page—you'll take the time to write them a brief note thanking them for their guidance. You'll be surprised at the joy you'll bring into their lives.

For your writing:

There are alot of special
people in our lives - not
necessarily one influential
person - that we can learn
& grow from. It's ours for
the taking to open our mind
& heart to be able to grow
from each person + situation.

Day 17.
What Not to Do

"[H]how can you say to your brother, 'Brother, let me remove the speck that *is* in your eye,' when you yourself do not see the plank that *is* in your own eye? Hypocrite! First remove the plank from your own eye, and then you will see clearly to remove the speck that is in your brother's eye." (Luke 6.42)

Throughout these daily devotions, I've given many sets of advice and to-do lists. Today, I offer a checklist of what *not* to do while you're walking your healing journey. The following, titled "Recipe for a Miserable Life," is anonymous, and so much the better for it. I think we could all write similar lists— about others. Of course we see *their* self-centeredness. Our own lists would be like a mirror in which we see everyone else's faces reflected but our own. But Jesus admonishes you to "remove the plank from your own eye" before trying to "remove the speck that is in your brother's."

So, here's your "Recipe for a Miserable Life":

> Think about yourself.
> Talk about yourself.
> Use "I" as often as possible.
> Mirror yourself continually after the opinion of others.
> Listen greedily to what people say about you.
> Expect to be appreciated.
> Be suspicious.
> Be jealous and envious.
> Be sensitive to slights.
> Never forget a criticism.
> Trust nobody but yourself.
> Insist on consideration and respect.
> Demand agreement with your own views on everything.
> Sulk if people are not grateful to you for favors shown to them.
> Never forget a service you may have rendered to someone and never let them forget it, either.
> Be on the look-out for a good time for yourself.
> Shirk your responsibilities if you can do as little as possible to get by.
> Love yourself supremely.
> Be selfish.

17. It's Your Turn to Reflect and Write. Throughout this seventeenth day of devotion, your task is simple: look back over the instructions given in "Recipe for a Miserable Life."

And don't do them! Toward the end of the day, ask yourself, "How did you do?" Then write out your answer.

For your writing:

Day 18.
"This Too Shall Pass"

The young parents were worried sick over their lost boy. They had gone with a group of friends to the big city for the holiday, as all the country folks do; and when they left for home, their twelve-year-old son wasn't in their van. They assumed he was riding with an uncle or cousin, but when the "family convoy" turned off the highway into a rest stop, he was nowhere to be found. Terrified, they sped back to the big city to hunt for him. For three days they searched, and the constant worry took its toll. They feared that they might never find their child.

But a shock awaited them when they reached the inner city. Everybody on the street knew about a boy who, on his own, was in the holy place of worship. And that's where they found him, sitting in the midst of politicians, physicians, priests, and philosophers—and they were taking notes on the boy's teachings! Imagine that: a twelve-year-old teaching the city's educated and elite. The parents fussed at him, but they really didn't know whether to scold or admire him.

Of course, I'm remembering Luke 2.41-50, where the twelve-year-old Jesus tarries in Jerusalem to "be about [His] Father's business," teaching in the Temple. There, Jesus the lost-finder is considered the lost one.

And the moral of this story? Even Jesus caused stress and worry on his parents.

I've heard it said that worry is like a rocking chair: it will give you something to do, but it won't get you anywhere. This is so true: we're stressed by the sheer busyness of life. We're always trying to make time where there is none left over. We even stress over our precious "down time," racing off to the gym for a frantic 45 minutes of aerobics before our next meeting. The stress shows up in the way we walk, the way we talk, the way we sleep (or don't sleep), the way we drive, the way we gulp down our food. It shows up in every aspect of our daily lives.

And when the stress builds up to boiling, we cry out for help.

A kindly old lady heard her phone ring and she picked up the receiver. She heard a young woman's voice on the other end but, without even a "hello," the young woman launched off into the troubles of her day. The laundry was piling up, the dishes in the sink were dirty, the kids were crying, and the husband wouldn't be home for hours. "Do you remember," said the young woman, "you told me when I was having one of those days that you, my mother-in-law, would come over and help me?"

So far, the older woman had been listening patiently. At last she said, "Honey, I think you must have the wrong number. I don't have any daughter-in-laws."

The stressed-to-the-max mother paused, then replied, "Well, haven't you ever wanted a daughter-in-law? Would you come over and help me anyway?"

It's good to cry out for help when needed, and we should turn to our friends and family members, of course. But, in the end, it's God whom we should turn to, "for your Father knows the things you have need of, before you ask him" (Matthew 6.8). He alone can return calmness and common sense to our hectic lives.

I hope that, by this eighteenth day of your journey, you've found peace in your daily "walk and talk" with God. I've learned that nothing is more calming, more restorative to the spirit, than a daily devotional. But still there are stresses surrounding you in daily life, and you need to practice turning those stresses around. Slow down and prioritize: not everything is a matter of life or worry.

There's an old Jewish saying commonly ascribed to Solomon: "this too shall pass." Remember that when you're being hit by stress: "this too shall pass."

Above all, stop worrying!

And think on this: when its letters are turned around, "STRESSED" becomes "DESSERTS." And without all those worries taking up your time and energy, you'll have more time to enjoy the sweeter things in life.

18. It's Your Turn to Reflect and Write. Throughout this eighteenth day of devotion, work on identifying and eliminating the stresses that continue to clutter your daily routine. For each stress that comes to mind, say to yourself, "this too shall pass." Find a quiet place and think on the good things in your life; then ask God to help you walk through the tough times.

And then get a good night's sleep. In fact, plan your bedtime ritual: get some bath salts and prepare for a long, relaxing soak in the tub. Things are sure to look better in the morning light.

For your writing:

As a reminder to reflect and
pause during others to see
what is really the root cause.

I worry
about things
that aren't worry
worthy!

Day 19.
The Miracle of Shoes

How beautiful upon the mountains
Are the feet of him who brings good news,
Who proclaims peace,
Who brings glad tidings of good things,
Who proclaims salvation,
Who says to Zion,
"Your God reigns!"
(Isaiah 52.7)

There are foundational moments in each of our lives, moments that, no matter what happens later on, we'll always remember those times when we knew something special happened—something unseen or inexplicable but real. We build faith on those foundations; they help us cope in our world of change and uncertainties.

I remember one such moment, which taught me that every event anywhere, everywhere, has a reason for its happening, whether any of us ever know it or not.

Essentially, what I learned in that crystalline moment was that God—always—has everything planned, and that it's my job to move in accordance with His plan.

For some days prior, I felt weighed down. It was nothing tragic or bigger than I could bear, but it was if the ordinary cares of life had piled up into a heap—which I was supposed to move by myself. And I had let these cares build up to the point that I wondered if God (or anyone else) really knew or cared. So I retreated into my office, closed the door, plopped down in my chair, and had a self-inflicted pity party with three in attendance: Me, Myself, and my good old friend I.

Well, the phone rang (of course!), interrupting my self-pity. It was a lady from Northside Assembly. "Pastor," she began, "this is a real off-the-wall request, but can the church use some shoes? I have quite a few pairs to give away."

I rubbed my eyes. "Sure," I said, "bring them over." Anyone who has had a yard sale knows that when shoes are worn out, that's when they're given away. *Right!...*

As I hung up the phone I thought to myself, *If these shoes are worn out I guess I can throw them away as easily as someone else can.*

An hour later, in walked this lady who attended our church. In her arms she carried a big box filled to the brim with shoes. "Here," I said, "let's just put this down by my office door."

"Thank you," she answered. Straightening up, she stared at the box—a bit awkwardly, it seemed. "Pastor," she continued, "I should tell you … these are not your typical shoes. They're very good shoes—I mean, they're expensive and good as new. But every pair is the same size, and it's an odd size, too."

"Oh?"

"Yes," she said. "They're all size one."

"What?"

She repeated it. *Who wears a size one?* I thought to myself. I thanked her for her generosity and proceeded to forget about the box of size one shoes resting by my office door. Needless to say, her gift did little to improve my mood.

I don't remember how much time passed, but the phone rang and a kind if unfamiliar voice was on the other end. And that's when the foundational moment happened.

"Pastor," she said, "you don't know me. I just moved into the neighborhood a few days ago and I have a request, a strange one, to ask of you." I assumed she was going to ask about our programs for youth and children or our community out-reach. "I've been praying to God to help me ..."

"Yes," I said, encouragingly, "... to help you how?"

"... I've been praying and asking to God to give me a new pair of shoes. I don't even know why I'm calling you and this church ..."

"—Well, we *are* in the SOUL business!" I said, being witty of mind. (Get it? Soul/sole ...)

"But you don't understand," she continued. "It's almost an impossible request. I need a size one."

I almost fell out of my chair.

"Lady," I croaked, "*you* don't understand. God has gotten you a pair of shoes. No: God has a whole box full of shoes for you. And they've been here, waiting just for you, and every one of them is a size one. All you have to do is come here and pick them up."

 It wasn't long before we were in my office together, standing over this box brimming with shoes, each a size one, tears streaming down our cheeks. And we knew that each shoe meant that GOD KNOWS, AND GOD CARES, AND THAT GOD DOES WHAT IS NEEDED TO MEET OUR NEEDS.

Now, you could say that the church helped her, but the fact is that she helped me:

> She needed shoes; I needed encouragement.

> She needed specially-sized shoes; I needed special proof that God knows and cares.

> She needed shoes to help her walk; I needed help in my walk with the Lord.

When I think back on this foundational moment, I'm reminded to stay open to God, to stay working and moving no matter what is raining down outside—or inside.

And, since that moment, I've stayed true to my resolution: no more pity-parties for Me, Myself, and I.

19. It's Your Turn to Reflect and Write. Throughout this nineteenth day of devotion, reflect on that foundational moment when you knew, just as Isaiah knew, that "Your God reigns!" Reflect on your walk with the Lord, and how he continually surprises you.

Understand that the path of healing does not exempt you from working in the world, with all its cares; rather, it changes your *relationship* to the world and your work and all its cares. There's no time for self-pity when you're working and moving with the Lord.

And remember: when you do something good for someone else, you're doing something good for yourself. And you're doing something beautiful *for God.*

For your writing:

Reminder that even
the smallest gestures
can change someones
day – a touch, smile,
doesn't always have
to BE <u>something</u>.

Day 20.
Big Tom!

"Therefore do not worry, saying, 'What shall we eat?' or 'What shall we drink?'… For your heavenly Father knows that you need all these things. But seek first the kingdom of God and His righteousness, and all these things shall be added to you." (Matthew 6.31-33)

The family that eats together usually stays within budget on food, but the family that prays together usually stays together. And my family prayed together so often it was like second nature. My parents were very loving and giving, and they modeled for us children what loving and giving can look like in the world. Whenever my parents saw opportunities for our family to give of our time, our abilities, or our substance or sustenance, all of us kids acted as one in support of their decisions—without questions, grumbling, or long faces.

I remember one Thanksgiving week when my parents were planning a nice, sit-down dinner for Friday. Me? I was floating around all day with visions of turkey legs dancing in my head. I looked forward to the ceremonial carving of the turkey, when the knife blade crackled through the taut, brown skin and the juices came tumbling out; to the mashed potatoes swimming in gravy; to the homemade creamed sweet corn; and to the yeast rolls straight from the oven—so hot and fresh that they steamed when you broke them open. And oh, yes, to mother's coconut cream pie. As my mother cooked and baked, the amassed smells of a roasted turkey dinner wafted through the house.

But later that afternoon, something happened. There was a new family we had come to know, and my parents learned that this family needed our meal more than we did. So mother finished up the cooking and packed it all up—every last morsel of it. We loaded it in the car and took our Thanksgiving dinner to a family that was much less fortunate than we.

We felt so good about what we had done. And as we got back home and walked through the front door, the aromas of Thanksgiving surrounded us. How were *we* going to celebrate? That's when father motioned us to hold hands and we bowed our heads; we gave thanks to God for His great bounty that comes in so many, many different forms.

Then he herded us into the kitchen for sandwiches and sent us to bed. As I went to sleep, I was haunted by the smells of what could have been my supper.

But in the wee hours of the morning I was startled awake. *Was someone at our door?*

I tried to stretch out my ears, listening intently. Sure enough, there was a soft tapping, like a child's hands patting at the wood. I waited, listening carefully. It happened again—a soft knock, or maybe the flat of a hand.

I slipped out of bed and crept to the door, still listening. Again came the soft tapping, and then a low, guttural mumbling. Trembling, I drew back the side curtain ever so slightly to look out—but there was nobody at the door. I heaved a sigh and slipped back in the darkness to my room.

I was back in bed when I heard it again—the same low mumbling, as if speaking softly just above a whisper.

Yes, someone or something was surely at our door.

I hurried to my parents' room and shook my father awake. "Dad!" I said. "Somebody's at the door!"

"You dreamed it, son. It's dark and there's no one out there. Go on back to bed," he said, and that was that.

But I didn't go back to bed. Instead, I went to the front door—and I heard the sounds, again. So I headed back to my parents' bedroom.

"Dad," I said, "I really think you ought to come and listen."

When my father went to the door he didn't pause to listen, he just opened the door wide and looked out. And the next thing we knew, a real live turkey came strutting in through the door and past us into our home. We followed him into the kitchen. I'm convinced that, if my dad hadn't finally caught Big Tom, he would have swaggered right over to the pots and pans, pried open the cabinet with a claw, flipped out the roasting pan with his beak, preheated the oven, salted and peppered himself, and jumped right in. All in the most dignified manner, of course.

Well, suffice it to say that Big Tom, Big Dad, and Little Me made such a racket that we woke up the whole family. My brothers and sisters each popped through the doorway and laughed, but when my Mother came in she stopped in the kitchen doorway, took one step backwards, then one step forwards, then covered her mouth with one hand: "Turkey? *We've got turkey?* Oh, my, we've got turkey!"

Without question, that Thanksgiving was the most blessed and the most memorable holiday we all spent together. When we sat down that evening to our Thanksgiving dinner, we tried to figure it all out—the hows, the whys, the wherefores. Our best guess was that the turkey got loose from a farm delivery truck. But it's an undeniable fact that Big Tom came to *our* house, to *our* door, to *our* table.

When I think back on that night, what amazes me is that Big Tom seemed actually to be knocking at our door; and when nobody answered he waited there, scratching and gobbling away until someone came to let him in. It's like he even knew where to go once the door was opened. He was on a mission, it seems.

At times like that, all I know is that you say grace and you really mean it.

20. It's Your Turn to Reflect and Write. Throughout this twentieth day of devotion—the next to last on your three-week spiritual journey—I invite you to give thanks to God for all His goodness.

Throughout the day, say grace like you mean it.

We would all die spiritually without God's grace, which in the New Testament Greek is *charis*, meaning "gift." We don't merit or earn our salvation: it's not a reward or payment but a true gift of which we are unworthy, and so we give thanks for His saving grace, just as we give thanks for all God's blessings and benefits and mercies and sustenance. And when we "say grace," that's what we're doing: "grace" here comes from the Latin *gratias*, meaning "thanks." As Paul writes in 1 Thessalonians 5.16-18, "Rejoice always, pray without ceasing, in everything give thanks; for this is the will of God in Christ Jesus for you."

And that's your task for today: "in everything give thanks."

For your writing:

pg. 137 - God is always at the door of our heart, & mind & prayer. HE is always there for us but we let worldly things get in the way of time. If we always go to Him 1st then, we'd spend less time + headache trying to figure this world out!

Also, being thankful of all things. Sometimes there are dark times + bewilderment but be thankful for what God brings you to & thru!

Day 21.
House of Hope Ministries

Congratulations on completing your third week of journeying! I have a special devotion to share with you on this special day, a shining example of how a church—and the people who worship in it and lead it and serve in it—can make a difference in the community. While pride of self is a deadly sin, it's with boldness that I declare my fatherly pride in the Northside Assembly of God, the church that I have pastored for the last thirty years.

Thirty years might seem like a long time, and you might think that a body would fall into a routine at some point and start taking things for granted. But every day is a new day for me at Northside Assembly. I feel the Holy Spirit moving among us as an enlivening, energizing power; and though I age in body, this church has kept me youthful in spirit. I love Northside Assembly and its people, who have become my family in the Lord; and I love what we have built together and how we have grown together under the Lord's guidance; and I give mighty thanks to God for having called me to His service in this church.

A few years back, Northside Assembly had the permit in hand to tear down a house just to the south of our Family Life Center. But God had plans to rebuild that old house, plans that included re-building lives that were broken and, seemingly, of little worth from the high cost of living in sin.

I was sitting in my church office when a husband and wife team came in and said, "Pastor, we want to minister to hurting women. All we need is a building to minister out of."

So I showed them the house that we were planning to tear down. They understood that there was a lot of work needed to save the old house, but they were wanting to use it for the Lord's work, so I brought their inquiry to the church's Board of Deacons. "Put a new roof on it without cost to the church and we will consider the request," was the Board's wise judgment.

When an old house falls into disrepair, it's the roof that goes first. Rain water starts leaking in, compromising ceilings and walls. Soon the whole house is moldy and unfit for habitation. It's like the progress of sin, when you I think about it. Isaiah speaks prophetically of the renewal of God's chosen people:

[T]hen the LORD will create above every
dwelling place of Mount Zion, and above her
assemblies, a cloud and smoke by day and the
shining of a flaming fire by night. For over all
the glory there will be a covering. And there
will be a tabernacle for shade in the daytime
from the heat, for a place of refuge, and for a
shelter from storm and rain. (Isaiah 4.5-6)

Cleansed of sin, his people will find "shelter
from storm and rain." But sin continues to take
us out from under the Lord's protective cover,
leaving us out in the cold and rain. And soon, like
a weather-beaten old house, *we* become unfit for
habitation.

But that broken-down house, once slated for dem-
olition, was getting a new lease on life: just a few
months later, the old roof was torn off and a new
one put on. And the total cost to the church was
$107, which went to feed a crew of seventeen vol-
unteer workers for a day. Otherwise, everything
had been donated.

And then, after some interior remodeling, that
old building was ready to become the House of
Hope, a transition program ministering to women
recently placed on probation or finishing rehab.
Much like the house they were now staying in,

these women needed to "clean up and rebuild" their lives, both in body and in spirit.

It's not a permanent home for them. House of Hope is a year-long program that combines instruction in life-skills with intensive Bible study—which is, of course, the most important life-skill of all. In time, "cleaned up and rebuilt," these women will set out on their paths, freed from the addictions that had bound them.

We know, and the city of Springfield knows, that House of Hope Ministries does much good: so much good, that we've grown to four houses—and we hope to add more.

It's such a joy to watch once-broken women transform into mature, responsible, successful members of our community. When a graduate of our program gets a job or her own home, we know Whom to thank: it's God's work that's being done in the House of Hope. And the primary means of their transformation, which volunteers from Northside Assembly lavish on these women in abundance, is love.

And the best is yet to come!

21. It's Your Turn to Reflect and Write. Throughout this twenty-first day of devotion, reflect on the times when you've sought shelter from storm, whether physical or spiritual (or both). We may move from town to town and from house to house, but still there's only one constant shelter in life, and that's the spiritual tabernacle of the Lord.

This is a good day to add volunteerism to your healing journey: if you don't already serve others in some capacity, then you're missing one of the true Christian blessings in life.

You might also do a "home inspection" of the sort that Paul implies in 1 Corinthians 6.19. You know that your body is "a temple of the Holy Spirit." So if you're still abusing or neglecting it in any way, then now—right now—is the right time to make that admission and "come clean." If you suffer from an addiction of any sort, please don't hide it any longer from yourself and from others. Give yourself back to God and seek help. (In fact, call us at church.) As Paul writes in Ephesians 5.17-21,

> And do not be drunk with wine,... but be filled with the Spirit, speaking to one another in psalms and hymns and spiritual songs,... giving thanks always for all things to God the Father in the name of our Lord Jesus Christ ...

And if you're feeling feistier in body and spirit today—which is a goal of these daily devotions—then by all means add "psalms and hymns and spiritual songs" to your to-do list. Turn on a Christian radio station, for example …

At Northside Assembly, our musical worship team rocks! But if you like the old gospel hymns, here's a "chestnut" by Vernon Charlesworth, composed in 1880:

> Oh, Jesus is a Rock in a weary land,
> A Shelter in the time of storm.
>
> A shade by day, defense by night,
> A Shelter in the time of storm;
> No fears alarm, no foes affright,
> A Shelter in the time of storm.

If you know the tune, then don't be ashamed to hum it or sing it out loud …

For your writing:

Whether you've reached a "rest stop" or an end indeed, I honor you for the journey you've undertaken. I give thanks to God that I, too, have walked much of the path you've just walked. I thank Him for having given me this chance to share with you some personal experiences and insights.

Do give thanks to God for being your traveling companion throughout these 21 days and for sending His angels to protect you. (You've practiced giving thanks on day 20, so you should be expert at it by now.)

And then, after you've made your thanksgiving, remember to forgive yourself. Self-forgiveness is among the hardest lessons, even for a pastor. But do learn to forgive yourself, even as God has forgiven you in Christ. Literally, "to forgive" means "to let go of" or "give up" some claim or debt. So "let go and let God." I used that last phrase as a chapter title and I'm sure you've heard it before; it might even seem a bit "tired," as if repeated a few times too often. But perhaps it resonates more deeply, now that you've practiced journeying with Him close by your side. The fact is that no phrase is trite if it speaks a truth about God. So, *let go …*

And I'd remind you, finally, that while our 21 days of devotion have ended, your spiritual path continues to unfold before you. So I repeat the wisdom of Proverbs:

> Trust in the Lord with all your heart,
> And lean not on your own understanding;
> In all your ways acknowledge Him,
> And He shall direct your paths.

A Blackard Family Postscript:

Through the following paragraphs, Pastor Alvin's family members offer their own words of thanks and appreciation.

From wife Susan:

My darling Alvin, it's not the number of words but their sincerity that declares one's true feelings. So I thank God for you. And I thank you. I admire you. I accept you. I rely on you. I trust you. I delight in you. And I love you, my dear best friend.

From son Nathanael:

Dad, you're my best friend. You're what I strive to be like. You always have an answer, and you always get things done. And through it all, you never complain. I love you and thank God every day for you.

From daughter Anna LaDawn:

You are mighty as a massive oak. You give shade to anyone in need. You are rooted in faith and love. You can hold up heavy loads and adapt to every changing season. You let people climb up and see the world from your higher perspective. And you never stop growing in Christ. Thanks for being the best dad God made!

From son Christopher:

To my dad,
As I live out my faith—
   you show me authenticity.
As I commit to my wife—
   you prove being steadfast.
As I teach my children—
   you are my example.
As I strive to be the man I desire—
   you teach me.
As my friend—
   you are constant.
As I am your son—
   you love me.

CPSIA information can be obtained at www.ICGtesting.com
Printed in the USA
LVOW11s2129281115

464009LV00004B/5/P

9 780982 818480